Blood Luxury

Poems

Ewuare Osayande

Africa World Press, Inc.

P.O. Box 1892
Trenton, NJ 08607

P.O. Box 48
Asmara, ERITREA

Africa World Press, Inc.

P.O. Box 1892
Trenton, NJ 08607

P.O. Box 48
Asmara, ERITREA

Copyright © 2005 Ewuare Osayande

First Printing 2005

Cover and Book design: Dapo Ojo-Ade

Library of Congress Cataloging-in-Publication Data

Osayande, Ewuare.
  Blood luxury : poems / Ewuare Osayande.
     p. cm.
  ISBN 1-59221-405-3 -- ISBN 1-59221-406-1 (pbk.)
  I. Title.

PS3615.S266B58 2005
811'.6--dc22

                              2005029286

for Shango & Sowande

and a new world
that must come
if we are to survive

Contents

Introduction vii

A Defiant Grace 1

BUCK 3

The Underground Railroad 9

In Some Churches and Mosques 15

ALWAYS OPEN SEASON 17

Aint Nuttin Butt Hoes & Trick-nology 22

for those with the ears to hear 25

Black Women Are Black Too 30

Must Be the Shoes 31

Patriotism Imported 36

and you wanna wave the flag 37

One Woman One Vote 38

strange weather 41

"I Speak of Freedom" 43

The Grateful Dead? 46

ANTHRAX ATTAX 47

When a Poem Is Feared More than a Bomb 53

ORIGINAL BORN 55

"His Master's Voice" 57

The Necessary Prerequisite 60

Supposed Rites 62

A Lynch Mob in the Sky 64

Matricks 1: Bullet Time 66

When we will forgive Trent Lott 67

Home 71

a face of flint 73

99 Problems & Jay-Z Is Just One 76

Identity Theft 80

Bling-Bling 85

Still Burning 91

Purely Victorious 94

INTRODUCTION

What a title! To seek in it, after it washes over and through you. That combining and overrunning relatedness. Blood as Blood, itself, a toxic swagger let out as it mostly is everywhere, not anymore as much some life circulating fluid.

Or Blood as stole in. To Be, then, "The Blood" as we is called amongst we... (and even A Gang - past tense of going, i.e. gone) We are most familiar these days with the Blood of vampire Killer appetite Bush Fiends. Definitions summarize power, place, energy.

To run that into "Luxury" is to make an image of exquisite "insanity." Like the "Caucasian Crib" where Wheaties (sp?), d cereal killers, lives. What kind of hideous "Light" seeps out, Luxor was "the light of the world" Elegba left the "y" to question.

Ewuare is young, strong-minded, full sensed and aware and yet aware he must get to wear the world like an inside the head & heart stocking cap. The outrage is the opening of the senses to reality. The dismissal of "The Given."

So begin with "A Defiant Grace," another wonderful title (to Gwen Brooks), then to "Buck" (Dolor is pain and literally Bread FR◇SP, depends on the accent).

What makes for the strength of the young poets seeing is the constant reference to struggle, linked to a ubiquitous continuum of doubt which is the only "dignity" the slave has. Yes, Buck the system, but know that it must be finally destroyed. As any such "liberation" within it is just a dance step, necessary, difficult, sometimes exhilarating but if not understood as "a stage" becomes a twist.

If we past being outright Chattel, how come the whole two cents never got here. If 89.9% Bloods "voted" (we know that's a lie), they thought, against Bush, then 1.01 has been copped, and we still has not received all our sense. and remains at 3.9. But at least, you say, we aint wooden Negroes who is only 3 cents whom E refers to, the "Hoes" found in all sexes.

What makes the book alive is that at each turn the poet reaches to grab the ugly and wrestle with it. And as contrast/contradiction to DuBois-Keats' "Truth & Beauty." For instance, sensitive to "the woman question" and how well paid "Hoes" have contracts to demean Black women. He says the women "the sistah" (the Black Man)" harassed /is Black/ too" so saying, the old cultural nationalist saw of African Traditionalism covering Male Chauvinism is pierced.

We won't go on, just to say that Ewuare is like the image Mao posed about Revolution, a ship yet some distance away, but whose tall and inspiring sails are already visible. Or as my ultimate artist-philosopher-teachers, T Sphere Monk said, upon visiting one of my out painter friends, "Man, you in a tough bi'nezz." So, say that for the poet, or the one who carry the RAZOR (Revolutionary Art for Cultural Revolution). Take this book as this brother's imposing sail, already aware of how to use the turbulence of the crooked to give fuel to his focus.

One more word, check the poem "It Must Be the Shoes" re: not only Error Jordan, but of the heaping compost of nouveau coon petty and comprador Zapalote who ironically, but quite scientifically predictable*, have grown big butt stomachs on their "next!s" as a result of the peoples struggles, and whose gig is now to suppress, silence, sit on and lie to us. This work, already passed around by mouth, based on this poet's hot Djeli Ya…is , in its solid composition, it's raging metaphor, it's relentless ideological (class) analysis, is one coming attraction of how tough this lad gonna be. The Goodest Knews is that Ewuare is one of a dozen or so really significant younger Djali who seem to know where they wants to go, in fact they is already going…and got a RAZOR in each hand!

Amiri Baraka
Newark Schools' Poet Laureate & The Last Poet Laureate of New Jersey

(*See Lenin, Vol 15, 18, *Collected Works*, "How Liberalism Separated from Democracy")

A Defiant Grace

for Gwendolyn Brooks (1917-2000)

you
Harlem Renaissance child
you
Langston's lil' sis
you
word-seamstress
created patchwork quilts
to bring comfort to the afflicted

god-mother of the Black Arts Movement
guided strident Black griots to sharpen their (s)words
readying them to do battle
showing them by your example
that commitment to community is what counts

you
sparked by the Molotov cocktail spirit of the moment
took your Pulitzer and popularity
and walked defiantly
out the front door
of the publishing house
that owned your work
and railed a broadside against America
and named it Riot

oh the accuracy of your words
the acute agony you articulated
the precise pain you penetrated
the loud love you lauded
the quiet contemplation you captured
and shared

in you was no need to boast
in being Black
just be
just be Black
and the brilliance will fall down off your back
like the shimmer from stars shooting across midnight skies
just be Black
relate to what is good
and resist what aint
is what you left us

elegant as an Ella Fitzgerald ballad

you
dignity defined
a defiant grace
skin
black and smooth as onyx
like your words
lil black stones
hurled at the Goliath
that defies our God
and denies our godliness
stones taken from the brooks
that is you.

BUCK

$@*%!

we are the BUCK$
from which they make the change
we never see

primitive
  capitalism
    primitive

born from between our momma's thighs

                    SPAWNED

from the jism of racism and sexism

                              class is colored!

        made over into money :: the loot exchanged for their luxury

        nigger coonery   issssssssssss   black currency

                    BLACK GOLD
              mined from West African shores
                    CONGO COINS

                        exchanged before there were
                            dollar dollar bills, yall
                    we was owned by the dead presidents
                            we work for now
                              we was
                        the cash they captured
                        the scrilla they secured

3

the paper they pursued
the cheese they chased
the benjamins they were about
we was their m-o-n-e ... why?
cuz we wuz
nickel&dimed outta our lives
we were the capital in capitalism
the product in the production of their bourgeois worldview
where being white could have some social value
international trade was made on us
multinational corporations and globalization
are just fancy words
for what we went through
the triangular slave trade
rum for sum Africans for sum cotton for sum rum
from Europe to Africa to the Americas

imperialism by any other name ...

before Wall Street was
we were the stocks traded
on markets called

AUCTION BLOCKS

no embargoes til 1812
stopped our human cargo
in slave ships stacked
our very Blackness commercialized

how slavery was defined

breeding plantations
an entrepreneurial wet-dream
rape as means to keep the supply in check

to meet the demand for more field-hands

cotton-pickers&tobacco-strippers
working under the all-seeing-eye of the whippers

two of the biggest industries this nation's ever seen:

Cotton, Inc.
the fabric of our lives

and R. J. was our massa from way back in the day

America in the black is more than metaphor
is irony sick and twisted
we have carried this economy
on our back sides
our black hides
since it was just a colony

America's property
federal reserve negroes
black capital
the means by which they make their ends
real estate
the original cyborg
not science fiction but political scientific fact
3/5 human
2/5 machine
for tax purposes our humanity was demeaned

business was very personal
our very persons

Massa's Cards
walking credit

with the signatures of our slave-masters
branded into our skin

the bar-code of bigotry

BUCK$
is what they called us
money
the root of all evil
is what they did to us
EVIL

they cha-chinged our lives away
like loose change
cashed us in as down payment
on their new world order

this is what they made us into
BUCK$
for their luxury
their very system survives
on our willingness to be their
BUCK$

to be the money they exchange
how they co-opt our culture
and change it into a commodity
for their entertainment
our culture is
our very existence
our very being
our very lives
this is how capitalism thrives

BUCK$
is that what we are?

BUCK$
>who we be?

BUCK$
>it is how they see us!

then so be it
BUCK them!

BUCK BUCK BUCK

>buck the system

BUCK
>make them pay

BUCK
>the system

BUCK
>make them pay

BUCK
>they owe us the very existence of their economy
>their very livelihood

BUCK THEM!

boycott them with our very beings
take our bodies back from them
buck the system
cash out of their accounts
stop being held in check
BOUNCE!
break out
steal our selves
from off the shelves of the corporate marketplace
rob our culture back

BLACK!

BUCK THEM!

DIVEST
DIVEST

detest what they have done to us
and how we still suffer
we need sanctions
time to shut them down
til they pay us REPARATIONS!

BUCK THEM!

shut them down

buck the system

BUCK

...

> Let them know
> the BUCK stops here!

The Underground Railroad

the ground under our feet
was the tracks that led us to freedom

the ground under our feet
was the tracks that led us to freedom

ground under
ground under
ground under ground
under ground under
ground RailRoad

(humming "Wade in the Water")

Moses got her heat on her side
her metal rod to part the waters wide
to steal away
steal away
steal away plantation's prisoners
moseying on down to the river
yes
aint no turning back Black
this here be a one-way ticket
outta the most wicked system ever devised
just keep yo eyes on the drinking gourd
and yo mind stayed on the Lord

the Underground RR
carrying a precious load
black gold
our human souls
spirit-combustion kept the train a-moving
this Soul Train

was not a Don Cornelius commercialized&commodified, pre-
fabricated, lip-syncing production
but this here train
was black-black
as black as Co(a)ltra(i)ne
engine screaming
bant baaaaaaaaaaaaaaaaaaaaaaaaaaaaaaaaaaaaaaaaaaannnnnnnnnnnn
nnnnnnnn
moving to a rhythm of a "Love Supreme"

doom   doom
doom doom
doom   doom
doom doom

with a Bessie Smith blues riff
belting out the smoke stack

had hell-hounds hot on our tracks
looking for familiar marks
on the barks of trees
ancient graffiti
aerosoled on the massa's mansion walls

we was "on the run
ducking the dog
and dodging the gun"

the Undaground
Nat Turner's hideaway
the Original Fugitive
holding council with Ogun
machete machinations
creating our own briar patch
where the lash couldn't catch us

be brer rabbit
outfoxing the fox
on his plantation
singing songs and pickin' cotton
all the while plottin rebellion

is John Henry
born with a hammer in his hand
an anti-capitalist metaphor for
Black labor against the corporate machine
laying down the rail
wailing like Fannie Lou Hamer
bout being tired of being sick and tired
refusing to lose
seeking refuge from water hoses and billy clubs
seeking refuge
for New World refugees
refused citizenry
Africa's dispersed and despised
a diaspora of outcasts and aliens
marooned on the island of invisibility
The Bermuda Triangular Slave Trade
paradise lost to pirates
with the skull and cross-bones of the Arawak and the Carib
buried in their flag
the Underground
where James Brown found
the Camelwalking across the Sahara
and talked that talk that only Fela Kuti could stand under
and dig
his way outta the quicksand of colonialism
and resurrect the sound of black rage
from Negritude to rude boy attitude
the link between Marcus Garvey and Bob Marley
there's a natural mystic blowing in the air

if you listen carefully now
you will hear
Garvey's ghost in the whirlwind and the storm
whistling Africa's redemption is near

and over here
Jimi Hendrix
takes his ax to the flag
reappropriating national sounds and symbols
with guitar picks and tongue licks
the stars for the ones we followed in our midnight flights
the stripes for the whips that marked our backs like branches
the red for our blood shed
the white is the color of our oppression
and the blues
the blues
is our indigo stained sorrow
hear him chopping down white cultural dominance
in 68 Olympic proportions
with the learned defiance
in Angela Davis' Black Power fist
that made the hit list
not Billboard's Top Ten
but the FBI's Most Wanted
the Undaground
as the Panther's lair
the railroad
how Assata escaped

is now hip hop running for its life
bleeding black feet frost-bitten
breakdancing in a winter wonderland
broken
being hounded by vanilla-iced snow men
and frosted m&m's

dreaming of a white Christmas
so they can unwrap rap
unwrap rap and
go diggin in the crates of our story
and sample our souls
and bite our very being

the Underground RR
is our culture
crying out to be free
in double-entendre self-determinations
is the mystery never solved
how these niggas still around
how we morph, adapt, change
and evolve and revolve and revolt
is the practice that precedes the theory

is the fact that we will never be satisfied
with not being free
that the train won't stop
til we is
free
til we is
free
til we is
see
getting to the North aint far enough

til we arrive at the station marked
"LIBERATION"

doom   doom
doom doom
doom   doom
doom doom

Ewuare Osayande

doom   doom
doom doom

Next Stop: Reparations

In Some Churches and Mosques

Black women can fill up the pews
but can't preach in the pulpit

hmmph!

Black women can usher in the aisles
but can't preach in the pulpit

welllllll!

Black women can pray at the altar
but can't preach in the pulpit

yall don't hear me!

Black women can cook in the kitchen
but can't preach in the pulpit

can I get a witness?

Black women can teach Sunday School

Lawd knows Black women teach Sunday School
but still can't preach in the pulpit

hmmmm …

wonder what would happen
if Black women left
and took their tithes&offerings
along with them …

and all God's people said

AMEN
     and
AWOMEN.

ALWAYS OPEN SEASON

1.

blood soaked
in the sin of a society
sick with the dis-ease of discrimination
and the denial of its own resident evil:

                        racism

you were caught
unprotected by your civil rights
under a hailstorm of semi-automatic acid rain
a bullet shower of forty-one drops of death
caused by the poisonous Gestapo gases
blowing out the ass-mouth of Rudolph Gulliani

you drowned in the flood of gun-fire
turned it to blood
this plague will persist
until America's hardened heart is broken
by us
and justice
        flows
              forth.

2.

Amadou
Amadou
Amadou
it was you
not your wallet
that posed a threat to them
the wallet was just a convenient cover-up

a white lie   an aryan alibi
for their calculated caucasian craziness
it was you
as in your Black skin
that provoked their paranoia
that led a lynch mob of forty-one bullets
to maraud&mangle your body
it was your Blackness
your dark skin
your ebony frame
that framed you

it could have happened to any of us
who are Black but
it was you
Amadou
and all they saw was your skin
the overseers gaze cast down on the enslaved
you are not the exception
        an isolated incident
your murder is the proof
and our lives testify to this truth
that justice turns her blinded eyes from seeing
that we are not free
we are still a colonized community
tied to the whipping post of the past
slave legacy lingers
like the stench of death
Dred Scott stares forth from your life-less eyes
our lives garner no respect

and so the system moved to the murderer's defense
but to this we scream: DEFIANCE!
we gave up the Sambo smile of submission
a long time ago

when we witnessed Emmet Till's mangled face
and watched his momma cry
something on our insides changed forever that day
we shed our fears
and unmasked our rage
no more running away
no more denying the reality of our oppression
no more making excuses
their insanity was now unacceptable

there is no other explanation
you can't rationalize racism
and it is this craziness
that colors the lens of our lives
and leaves us asking "why?"
and leaves our jaundiced eyes unable to find justice
it is this insanity
that creates the insecurity
that we carry in this country

it is always open season on us
we are walking targets
in occupied territory
a community under siege
with no refuge
no asylum
no amnesty
all we have is ourselves

but this evidence will not be entered into the judicial record
it won't even make the morning news
but it is this evidence on which we stand
and rest our case
of being born in the hue of our history
with the birthmark of fate

we bear the brand of those murdered because of our Blackness
a piece of us is buried with them
as we wrestle for some peace
in the coffins of our confinement
their spilled blood is pumping in our veins
for we are one
and we know we are right
no matter how many juries genuflect
to the wishes of white supremacy
we will never give up the fight
We Will Never Give Up The Fight
WE WILL NEVER GIVE UP THE FIGHT
for we know we are right
and we know who the real threats are

3.
the real threats
are they who are deadly
not because of their guns loaded with bullets but
because of their minds loaded with bigotry
minds manufactured in fascist factories
the same factories that created

slave ships
plantations
whips, chains and Jim Crow

reservations
scalping
diseased blankets and broken treaties

concentration camps
ovens
showers and the swastika

the opium wars
wage slavery
and the atom bomb

ghettos
barrios
shanty towns and sweatshops

prisons
the death penalty
three strikes and lethal injection

it is they who are the real threats
to society and civilization
it is they who have wreaked havoc on humanity
it is they who are the rapists, robbers and con-men of continents
the serial killers of the century
murderers of the millennium
it is they who are the real threats

it is they who deserve death.

Aint Nuttin Butt Hoes & Trick-nology

ad hoc to his story
stands the auction block
in retro shock
still got Black women's bodies
center stage
bidding their souls away
ridding them of their subjectivity
no longer whole
just hoes
to be bought and sold
post-modern plantation poster-girls
spread out world-wide
in everything from commercial ads to web-pages and porno rags
sex sells
and the bodies of Black women elicit the greatest demand
yet remain the least respected
their self-image distorted
their bodies contorted
twisted out of reality to fit the deranged consumer mind-set
by bounty-hunter photographers
searching for the biggest booty
to fetch the fattest paycheck
shootin Black women
shootin Black women
locked in their camera sites
graphed into photos
that become prototype
for how all Black women will be viewed
the image fixed and chained to the page
reproduced rapidly in the slave quarters of capitalism
pictorial property to be voyeuristically raped
by multi-culti mysognist massas
jungle bunnies hip hoppin

in white boy wet dreams brought to the wide screen
the great escape
Tarzan turns out Foxy Brown
right there in the middle of the stage
and its all the rage these days
to be Black, buck-naked and paid
to play the part of the Venus Hottentot
hot-to-trot Black ass in chains
untamed exotic caged in her mind
might be erotic to some
but sexism is the same by any other name

which explains why so-called video hoes
get hooked and reeled in by producer pimps
Black like they
but skin is thin when the cash is thick
getting paid to put their ass on display
but aint no amount of money can cover
the damage done to one lil Black girl
raised on rap videos and gangsta flicks
this aint nuttin butt hoes and trick-nology
disguised as neo-feminist ideology
by $-hungry misogynists
designed to crook Black women
into embracing the hooker-look
believing it to be an act of liberation
for Black female sexuality
but its just a tragic magic potion
that forces them to endorse their own demise

pop culture as pedagogy of the oppressed
miseducated on mediated images
living their lives based on lies told via the tv

we need to storm the hood with books by bell hooks
so sistas can find out
who was the thief
the con
the crook
that took their get-out-the-ghetto dreams
and turned them into get-rich-quick schemes
by conniving them into playing the sexual vixen
nixing the negative f/x of her representation
and how it connex
to the rate of rape, incest, domestic abuse, disease and death
effectively marginalized
so self-defined dreams are never realized
lives silenced
frozen in the photographic memory
of mammies and whores
where caricature covers the oppressive reality
and can't talk back
can't speak
their mouths muffled by the masking tape of masculinity
isolated in the video screen
where her-story is never heard
is never heard

blow the auction block to smithereens
so Black women's bodies will be demeaned no more
and their minds no longer caught in a state of shock
sold like livestock
going going
GONE.

for those with the ears to hear

STOP
Catch the world
as it spins on its axis
and ask yourself
"what do we need?"
then be it

think outside the box
be the alternative
to the alternative that aint
that's controlled by the same corporate dams
that dictate the flow of the mainstream
be an authentic voice
an authentic image
not a regurgitation of some momentary market trend
be unco-optable
no sell-out
or souled out
a self that can't be misinterpreted
misconstrued or manipulated

cuz being different aint enough
if you don't dare to divest
from forces that exploit
that oppress
that dress up colonialism and call it diversity
that turn difference into an exotic tonic
a drug to intoxicate our minds
and keep us transfixed
while they fabricate our past
and forecast our future
quit patterning yourself

after what you see on MTV or BET
Honey, VIBE and the Source are farces
controlled by faces that don't look like us
these rags don't represent you
but the interests of the advertisers
that line their pages
who seek to make a profit
from your internalized oppression
resist the stereotypes
they've created for you
rather
be the prototype
of what needs to be seen

recognize
how our lives have been inverted
and be the revision
that will revert the repression of our innate divinity
invent the reverse
that will take us back to the future
and move us forward
free
be the Sankofa bird
that truth that needs to be heard
be the Word
manifest in the flesh

be that truth that bends but not breaks
a truth that is not narrow
but broad and above-board
not dogmatic but dynamic

remember all the injustices that your people went through
in their quest to seen as human beings
and speak for all the times they were silenced

stand for all the times they were forced to sit in the back
out of sight   out of their minds
love for all the times they were hated (repeat)
it is their shed blood
that enables you to be
walk with their memory
NEVER FORGET
live with a profound humility
and an informed sensitivity
to how the past impacts our present
and sets the path for the future
then   step   into   tomorrow
anchored in the shore-ty of knowing
that our truth is non-negotiable
is not for sale
or deal-making in back-door smoke-filled rooms
with politicians or corporate execs
who seek to turn our experience into a marketing scheme
to achieve their American dream
that has the rest of us stuck in a non-stop nightmare

wake us up

conjure fury
and temper it with focus
and force them to face your justified rage

represent righteousness

be it
be that truth
that in yo-face truth
that sho-nuff truth
that proof that lies in the eyes
of all who suffer and resist

and rebel
and resist suffering
and rebel
who holler, scream and yell
who give their oppressors hell
for all the torture they received
who tell it like it is

be that truth
speak that truth
walk that truth
talk that truth
live that truth

be truth set aflame
name yo place
know the
who
what
when
where
why &
how

claim yo time

NOW

be blazing
blazing hot

light up the spot with your lives
so others can see a new way to be
outta the darkness of their dilemmas

conjure the courage

learn the skill

empower the will

seek serious solutions   to our ills

better still

BE the Revolution.

Black Women Are Black Too

The next time a Black man
cries racism
when accused of violating a woman
of the same hue
will someone please remind him
that the sistah he harassed
is Black
too

Must Be the Shoes

enter Spike Lee
playing a Blackman named Mars
like Marvin the Martian
homeboy from Outerspace
down to the sneakers on his feet
sneaking away from scrutiny
in a Nike commercial
muttering it
must be the shoes
must be the shoes
must be the shoes
yessir bossing his way to fame
& 40 acres of prestige
with Warner Bros. logo branded
into his mule's ass
flying on the heels of the world's
favorite nigga

Space Jam
Air Jordan
double dribbling on black boys' hoop dreams
of being like Mike:
NBA All-Star
multi-national product endorser
imperialism's colored spokesperson
smiling sambo on the tv screen
selling you shit you really don't need

"& he's up up up and away
this is incredible
he's amazing
super"

(and other white liberal superlatives of exotified glassy-eyed
admiration)
watch him on the instant replay
in slow motion
from behind the color line
as he defies gravity
and transcends his race
to become the most recognizable face on the planet
and
"damn that nig —
uh, I mean
that boy must have rockets in those shoes"

& Mars Blackman is heard mumbling
from behind the curtain

it must be the shoes
it must be the shoes
it must be the shoes

as the camera closes in on the sneakers on his feet
where his black shadow sits on the back as name brand
palming the brick
about to slam dunk
& smash in the faces of Southeast Asians
to cash in on a global sensation
&
SWOOSH!!!
he nets a profit of 20 million a year
just for putting his silhouette in flight
on a pair of Nikes
that acts as black shield for CEO Phil the white Knight
deflecting accusations of racism
as he jostles people of color in Third World countries
and here

yeah it
must be the shoes
must be the shoes
must be the shoes
that got them paying multi-national dues
slaving to the sewing machined rhythms of Southeast Asian
blues
said it must be the shoes

as Nike tells us
"Just Do It"
and they do

just exploit
just oppress
just enslave
just do it to death

but in Indonesia
lil brown boys don't wanna be like Mike
they hate Mike
and despise Nike
who own them and their families
paid slave wages
working for pennies in shops of sweat
in debt
their lives like the laces they thread
tied in knots
never to come loose
they work far away
from the sounds of screaming fans
and the media glare
no reporters will be rushing them at the half
to get a sound-byte for the 11 o'clock sports segment

for one
there are no time-outs there
no coaches but overseers
and no trainers to rub Ben Gay into sore muscles
or give them Gatorade
after 18 hour work days
and two
there work is survival
not like here
where we pay to watch overpaid athletes play
and three
there are no retirement plans
or contracts
or agents representing these families
who live in slums
where the sum value of their lives
is worth less than Shaq's Escalade

so you say the NBA is fantastic
but how can the revolution be basketball, KRS?
it seems knowledge aint supreme
when the truth is that
we can't find justice on the ball court
cuz the arenas are run by corporations
that practice savage capitalism
they won't get called for traveling
into other countries and buying out governments
where labor is cheap
while poor kids here
will never get paid a livable wage
to make the very sneaks
they beg and borrow to buy or steal
and why?
cuz all wealth is theft
mos def

don't be confused selling their shoes with our redemption songs
cuz when the whistle blows
there is only one winner
cuz our lives are always played under sudden death
and we don't get any free throws
cuz the refs are paid not to call the foul

yeah it
must be the shoes
must be the shoes
must be the shoes
cuz we the world over
who pay them dues
live them blues
continue to lose.

Patriotism Imported

and the Betsy Ross you honor
is now a Chinese woman
working 18 hr shifts in Shanghai
wiping the sweat from her face
with the fabric that will become the flag you wave
with pride

but how?

when you read the label and find
MADE IN CHINA

why
your patriotism isn't even American made.

and you wanna wave the flag

During WWII
German soldiers captured
sat their Nazi asses in the front
while their Black captors sat in the rear
of the bus

and you wanna wave the flag
and honor soldiers never honored at home

they returned not to ticker-tape parades
or presidential serenades
but lynch mobs, burning crosses
"yessir bosses" and their dignity robbed

we have fought in every war
for freedoms we have never experienced

the 1st to enlist
the 1st to die

why am I so incensed you ask?

on September 10th
I couldn't drive from Philly to New York
without being harassed.

One Woman One Vote

for Congresswoman Barbara Lee

and when the planes crashed
the whole nation shook
like a California earthquake
Richter Scale rage rippled from coast to coast
and when the smoke cleared
only one tree was left standing
you

rooted in your resolve
not swayed by the blind tide of revenge diatribes
of "somebody must pay"
taped to the back of some mad white man's Chevy van

and when you cast your vote
it was not lost in solitude
but was cast on behalf of we who believe too
and we all win because of you
420 to one
and the balance of justice
fell to your side
under the weight of your conviction

conscientious objector
conscious observer
you know that war can never bring the peace we seek
that just as the death penalty does not deter crime
war won't stop terrorism
you know
that peace without justice is oppression
camouflaged in the fatigues of social control

your moral compass
points due North to freedom
like the North Star did for Tubman
your roots planted deep in the river Jordan
she crossed for your namesake
Barbara

you say
honor the dead
not by killing more
but by stopping that which causes death
by honoring the sanctity of breath&bone
you defied those who worship gold, steel and stone
they cannot understand your language
for all the words on their tongue
translate to violence

but you
in your silence
speak a word understood in every language
down through the ages

peace

I call you sista and savior
for you have rescued truth, restraint and a people's dignity
from drowning in the gutter
of spit from the mouths of warmongers
who bask in the blood of humanity
for vanity

I see you
as you sing
this lil light a mine
I'm gonna let it shine

one solitary flicker struck
by the match of your conviction
has lit the candle of our confidence
renewed for the millions who call for no more war
holding onto the hands of Hiroshima's memory

shine on sista
shine on

to light us a pathway

home.

strange weather

we are the strange weather of autumn
the forecast is as fickle as the times

we feel the hurt
like the howling of the wind
the sadness in this season
the leaves fall like our tears
mourn for the loss of loved ones
the pain of this tortured existence
things haven't been well for some time
for most of us
we need not justify our actions
those who need to know
already understand

what matters
is that we love ourselves without apology
and that is a lot in itself
& at the same time
just the half
we still don't fully appreciate what that means
and so our pain multiplies
due to our willful ignorance at times
and greed disguised

truth is a lonely road
horde nothing
not even people
the times will probably get worse
before they get any better
gotta dig the trenches deeper
no one knows which way the wind blows

or what it will bring

the days are growing darker
sooner
the dead walk without peace
winter is coming
our discontent has already arrived
this weather is as strange
as we are in this land
we were never made for this climate
why are we told hell is so hot
when the darkness is so cold
our Hades is an inferno of ice&snow
we been frostbitten by bitterness

witness the signs of our mortality
etched in the earth
and as you store up food
again
store up love

start at home

and make no apology for that.

"I Speak of Freedom"*

for Kofi Annan

African Atlas
carrying the weight
of 4.5 billion lives
worldwide
on your shoulders

but who carries you?

you stand
on the stool
carved from the roots of your family tree

you are their libation
their blood
poured in the name of colonization
now flows in your veins

are you an ambassador of peace
or a comprador for the powers-that-be?

cease the deceit
untie the knot of lies
unite with the masses
not the magistrates who represent
the dollar, the euro or the pound

let your voice resound like King
bring truth to the world stage
quoted on the front page of the papers across the globe

disrobe the emperor
whose clothes are soaked with the blood of Baghdad

diplomacy should never be a handshake with death
this is no time for saviors or soldiers
peace is not a publicity campaign
but a process
meant to relieve the oppressed
from the burden of an unjust debt
thievery of a thousand years
of slavery and colonization

who ruled the world
now runs the World Bank
do they sign your paycheck too?

whose pepper stew
brews in your belly?

in what direction do you pray
toward the Vatican, Accra or DC?
God doesn't reside in bombs made by Lockheed Martin
but in the cries of children
in Iraq, North Korea, Cuba and Zimbabwe

how are we to trust you are working on the world's behalf
when you confer with international killers
who break treaties
before the ink dries
just ask the Cherokee
the Lenape
or the Sioux

defy them on the principle your grandmother taught you
from a tongue as old as the earth

in the end
how you got where you are
doesn't change the fact that you are there
and that there are billions of faces
looking to you through the eyes of Nkrumah
with only the red dust of their determination
in their hands
outstretched to you
with one demand

"I SPEAK OF FREEDOM!"

*The title of this poem comes from an address of the same name given by Kwame Nkrumah in 1961. Kwame Nkrumah is known for leading the anti-colonial struggle that would lead to the development of Ghana. He was also Ghana's first president.

The Grateful Dead?

you have no choice

there is no place for you to run

no refuge 'cept the afterlife

deathwish is all that is left
after life's dreams
have been demolished
by bulldozers driven by soldiers
who believe you are scum

and no matter how many white Gentiles
holding up peace signs
come wearing bright orange vests
to protect them from what you face each day
you know placing daisies in the rubble
will not stop the rampage

and your remains will not be remembered
by the Americans that will play "show&tell" on tour
showing their battle scars and shell-casings
sick souveneirs of their adventures in a real-life war zone
and they will pat themselves on the back with praise
for days on end

all the while you will be dead

and they will still expect you
to be grateful.

ANTHRAX ATTAX
"an unconfirmed report"

the air has been weaponized
scared to breathe
the slightest itch
a strange odor
got folk running to the CDC
for a report

gas masks make a mockery of the madness
ever try sleeping in one of those things?

Ted Kopple sits on Nightline
as the world topples
forgot to tell us that we wouldn't be in this mess
if America had signed the
Anti-Biological & Chemical Warfare Pact
way back in '72

as Americans sit eyes glued to the tube each night
unaware that
its the airwaves that are infected
information's diseased
polluted with spores
produced by the STD of media whores
inhaled via the tv &print media
intoxicate you with hysteria
got ya hallucinating
making you believe your free and secure
when you aint so sure

exposure to the tube
infrared ultra-violent rays that broad

cast a network-
ing to hook&reel us in
with the bait of bigotry

whipped into a frenzy
maneuvered into a position of fear
like a deer caught in the headlights
Americans rush to sign on the dotted line
giving up the only known hope for a cure
the bill of rights

a jingo aint a commercial ditty

but history is a re-run situation comedy
brought to you by
the makers of White House
instant democracy
no need for votes
just pour and stir

produces martial law
constitution suspension
rights on ice
govt sanctioned repression
the whole country is a concentration camp
fascism is back in fashion
McCarthy makes a comeback
gone retro
COINTELPRO reprise
the phantom of the Pentagon
Hoover haunts the halls of the FBI
I spy with my lil eye
the rise of the 4th Reich

freedom is fiction
democracy a fantasy

record breaking approval rating—
the whole country's gone postal!

The US notion of advancement:
from the Bionic Man to the Bionic Army
6 billion dollar defense

and the White House shuts up the press
don't play that mess
betta watch what you say and print
cause your dissent could be your descent

if headlines were honest
they would read
"The Far Right Unites"
white supremacists partied when the Towers fell
Christian and Muslim fundamentalists agree on the bottom-line
the Aryan Nation graduated in 89
from burning crosses to bombing abortion clinics
and subways with the Bubonic Plague

corporate drug dealers
push their products
on the corner of Wall Street
home test kits just in time for Christmas
Cipro becomes America's crack of choice

"All Hail the Chief of the World's Police"
if Rodney King were a Third World country
this government would be the LAPD

but we must remain loyal
must remain loyal

must remain loyal
to Bush
in his pursuit of more oil
for the family dynasty
but will someone please explain to me
why is Bush trying to kill his business partner
bin Laden
CIA Blowback
is this wack or what?

homeland security?
& for who?
for who?
when the first people here had their homeland invaded
security for who?
…
here
lemme give you a
klu

@ Ground Zero

the criminal plays hero
fiddling while NYC burns
blaming the Muslims
like Nero blamed the Christians
in Rome

@ Ground Zero
we are our people's only heroes
at the bottom's bottom
one with the soil
no stranger to toil or danger
laboring our lives away
born in war-zones

bombed-out homes
from city blocks to cell blocks
our lives are perennially patrolled

@ Ground Zero
where we reside
at the bottom of the rubble
buried beneath charred
steel,
flesh,
stone,
blood,
concrete
and bone
the stench of death floods the nostrils
holding on for dear life
the world's masses
enmeshed in a cacophony of mass confusion
crying out
DOWN HERE!
DOWN HERE!
but no one hears
us
no one hears
yet through all the sorrow
pain and fear
we will remain

there aren't enough of them
to destroy us
all

we
are the world's majority

Viet Nam proved he could no longer win a war on the ground
and after the last bomb has dropped
we will still be here

chanting down your demise

NO MORE LIES!
NO MORE LIES!
NO MORE LIES!

with a record of all the world's dead
with defiance in our fists
and their anger in our eyes.

When a Poem Is Feared More Than a Bomb

for Amiri Baraka

When words
   just   words
are WARRED upon

when A, B, C's are   SEIZED

and held hostage

syllables assasSINated

lingo lambasted by gringos

when vowels&consonants are constantly
being SHOT out the airwaves

when sentences are sequestered

when honesty is placed
under house arrest

when jargon is JAILED

truth TORTURED!

the facts have their assets frozen

 when eloquence is
ELECTROCUTED

when speech is spurned

then BURNED at the stake
when they take Reason
and call it Treason

when diction is disscredited
common sense CENSORED

when SANITY is straight-jacketed

 by the INSANE

when
they
ban
the use of
your
BRAIN!

then …
then …

THEN

you will realize
that

LIES RULE THE WORLD

and our minds
are more DANGEROUS
than all their damn land mines
        combined

ORIGINAL BORN
for Paul Robeson

he came   unchained

singing in the eye of the noose

no matter how twisted the knot
round his neck
he never choked back his words

vocal chords of steel
forged in the minds of Africans enslaved
the epitome of their will to be free

ORIGINAL BORN

they spit him out
blood sweat and tears
a talent and gift for every year under the whip

he carried their spirituals
from plantation fields to symphony halls
filled to capacity with the world's masses
dying to be freed
from similar masters

an ambassador of Blackness
the inversion of their madness
a renaissance in the flesh
running past white supremacy
in the 100 year dash
he was ahead of his time
for all times

for a time yet to be defined
a beauty too bold for certain eyes to behold
still

Jim Crowed
passport pick-pocketed by congressional hustlers
who called him communist
as if to curse him
cause he sought community with the world

they were scared of him
had to hush his mighty Black mouth
topple our ebony tower
our black fist before "Black Power"

they were scared of his vocal range
loud like a thunder clap
cracked the shackles of colonialism
his voice echoed the cry of 800 million worldwide
destined to win their freedom

the storm of his resiliency
kept Truman trembling under white sheets
peering out the White House window
into the midnight of his skin

"His Master's Voice"

the dog sat at attention
listening to his master's voice

his master's voice

were we better situated
than the mutt?

trained to sit when told
to speak when spoken to
never to look at them in their eyes
no
never do that

and never
ever
under any circumstances
were you to
think for yourself

or listen to your own voice

black migration
moving to the sound of the train
industrial age
mass exodus
from the sharecropping South
up north
in search of sovereignty

how the blues spread
from Mississippi to St. Louie
RCA wasn't too keen on hiring our kind
called us coons
while they robbed us blind
as Lemon Jefferson
but even he could see
that even after slavery
we still weren't free

they stole our sound
and pressed us into their vinyl

called it "race records"
more like racist wreckage
erasing the record of our humanity
turned it to minstrelsy

how you gonna copyright culture?
a people's way of being in the world

they bootlegged the blues
jacked jazz
burned the hot iron of ownership
into the backside of our souls

sold us lies
their contracts were them
conning us into allowing them to track our lives
leaving us nothing but the blues
that made the muse sick
so they could loot and lampoon our lyrics

twisted round our mouths
chalk lines of death

and named it "black face"
they amos and andied us
into a state of minstrelsy
that has become the cross-over
which we have been hung
and nailed
left to die

The Necessary Prerequisite

there is something to be said about sacrifice
about putting it all on the line
for the sake of a future
we may not see
and so when all the white kids were busy kissing toilets
after discovering how many kegs they could consume
or how many they could jam into a telephone booth

you were burning incense and midnight candles
contemplating action
that could cost you your education or your life
and all the hopes placed on you
for being the first in your family
to go to college

and if you told them your plan
they told you that you need to be grateful
but you were in pursuit
of a greater need

they didn't see what you saw
or how you saw it
from the vantage point of visionaries
and so on that day
as you walked out onto the campus green
and marched to the president's office
with your list of demands
having only your blunt determination
you weren't doing it for yourself
you were doing it for me

I know when you erected Black Studies departments
out of the sharecropper shacks
you weren't motivated by the delusion of inclusion
for wanting our story told in between lies
you wanted the facts to act as rod of correction
you quickened the resurrection of dissent
not just to complain
but to change our society

the necessary prerequisite for changing the world

Ewuare Osayande

Supposed Rites

I was a suspect long before they did a record check
arrested on false charges

an accusation is all it takes to put one's life in suspension

between hell and fate
prison is a pergatory
a Black man's supposed rite
but I don't subscribe to slavery

I was profiled
hunted down like the game that never wins
caught
cuffed
wrists twisted into knots

all my belongings left on the roadside

in the back of the squad car
at the mercy of two white men
wielders of a power they don't respect
who never met my sons or know my mother
who wouldn't know me from another brother

and they showed me my mug shot
as if to get my approval
while they chained me to the chair
like a restless rottweiler
to question me
and so I sat there
quickly aware that I was more intelligent than them both
as they replied with a politeness that was as plastic as their faces

telling me that this is all routine
the fingerprints
the hand cuffs
the accusations
the dehumanization

playing the role of the good cop
but stop
what is a good cop?
is that like a good enslaver?
a good massa?
a good trader?

what makes what they do good?
and had I not been able to make bail
the Black tax for living under a system that ain't your own
I would have been sent straight to jail
like my ancestors before me
I had buy my freedom
but it is only as temporary as today

A Lynch Mob in the Sky

and all the environmentalists are not tree-hugging whites
who want to save the whales
while the harpoon's sites remain trained on our backs

some of us are mothers fighting cancer
from living in neighborhoods
where plants are not green with leaves
but are toxic waste dumps made of lime and concrete
fighting death and disease
by teaching the people about environmental racism

we suck sewage every time we breath

live in strategic areas Superfund sites call
sacrifice zones
black canaries in racist white minds
the first to die
so they can have more time to escape
in case of a leakage or unexpected chemical outbreak

and we inhaled the governor's words
only to choke on her lies
like the pollution that it is

and we watched as she would become the head of the EPA
and wondered out loud

How?
Why?

while our children suck on nebulizers at night
just to breathe

and then one day we looked to the sky
and realized that the air had become a lynch mob
choking us daily
a slow asphyxiation
the klan turned in their sheets
and are now hiding behind puffy white clouds.

Ewuare Osayande

Matricks 1: Bullet Time

Morpheus
Morpheus
Morpheus

Where are you
when we need you most

too busy training
some white computer geek
while we get shot down in the street

bang bang bang bang bang
bang bang bang bang ...

imagine Amadou Diallo
dodging 41 bullets ...

BANG BANG BANG BANG
BANG BANG BANG BANG ...

we
are as Neo
as neo-colonialism.

When we will forgive Trent Lott

the hood has been pulled off
another racist been exposed
hosed down in the bile
of his own vile contempt
for social progress

but God bless

he now claims
he's seen the light
the error of his ways
on his way to the press conference
to ask for our forgiveness

it was a slip of the tongue
you say
a slip like a snake's lisp
your very presence is poisonous
is violence expressed
in legislative collar and tie

yr breath reeks of death
drink cocktails mixed with kerosene
fire-breathing Grand Dragon
Southern Black churches mysteriously burn
when you come to town

you say you're gonna change yr racist ways
throw a few votes across the tracks

honorary provost of Bobby Jones' university
yr body will play host

to Strom Thurmond's ghost
once he's finally deceased
to Strom Thurmond's ghost

how many more Black bodies have yet to be found
at the bottom of the Mississippi?

what would Fannie Lou
have to say bout you?

congressional aid to that Dixiecrat Bill Colmer that
refused her a seat at the Democratic Convention
back in 64

what role did you play
in making sure
Medgar Ever's murderers faced
an all-white jury?

why should we believe your story?

poverty pimp supreme
you sit behind your desk and day dream
of whips and chains
plantation fantasies
still haven't forgiven Lee
for surrendering the Civil War

race whore from the state
that didn't outlaw slavery til 1985

what was that?
an oversight?

the same reason why a confederate flag

still flies atop the Mississippi state house
is that an oversight too?
so you want to know
when will we forgive you

maybe it'll be after you reveal the names
of all the jack-asses and ivory tusks
that secretly hold your views too

or maybe we'll forgive you
after you have raised millions for Black farmers
a dollar for every cent you raised
for the Conservative Citizens Council
the group whose predecessor
funded the white terrorists
that bombed the Freedom Riders' bus

or maybe it'll be
after you've served time in the county jail
a year for every year you voted against King's holiday
and while there
we'll watch you beat yourself black&blue
a lick for every time the nightsticks hit Fannie Lou Hamer
leaving her crippled and blind in one eye

consider it a spiritual exercise
to purify you of any evil intent

and when you fall asleep
you'll have a vital organ removed
for all the Black women sterilized in your state
without their knowledge or consent
and when you awake and realize what you lack in your insides
you'll be informed that all the replacement donors are Black
what would you say to that?

maybe we'll forgive you
when the Klan has been banned
and all its members have been detained and deported
back to their ancestral homeland

or after we watch you burn Mississippi's confederate state flag
as you recite from memory
King's "I Have A Dream" speech
then go to every church in your region
and preach a sermon on the evils of segregation

or maybe it'll be
after you show up to vote
only to be told that you'll have to pass a poll exam
the first question being
"how many bubbles are in a bar of soap?"

maybe we'll finally say,
Lott, its all okay
the day your appointed president
signs into law the African American Reparations Act
that you will publicly support and work hard to pass
then hold his hands and sing "Free At Last"

and if you complain that this is unreasonable
that we're being unfair
that we are mongers of hate
we'll simply remind you of what you said in 81
in a Supreme Court brief
that "race discrimination doesn't always violate public policy"

maybe then
we'll forgive Trent Lott
but then again
maybe not.

Home

our homes were broken
on the auction block
when baba and iya had their child snatched
from their arms
her scent lingering in their embrace
their faces exploding in an ocean of tears
in silence

our families were never meant to function

but on freedom's eve
we weaved quilts
from the artifacts of our memory
and made a road map to tomorrow

on that day
we walked defiantly out of massa's gates
with only our faith as companion

the only thing on our mind
was finding kin and kind

with feet on fire
we walked for worlds
held our dignity close
right next to our emancipation papers
tucked between the whip marks
on our back

we saved our tears
for those we knew would
cup them in their palms

and promise protection
from the haints and horrors to come

we carry this history in our hearts
in our songs
in old postcards
in pictures that sit on the ledge of our legacy
with glasses of water
strange faces that look like our own
we carry this history in our memory

it matters not what those think
who drink from fountains
that did not welcome our thirst

what matters is that we re
member
continue putting ourselves back
to get her

what happened to us is beyond travesty
is the evil that still goes down around town

we resist this
by embracing those who would be snatched
by seeing ourselves in their faces
by telling them "I love you" for no reason
by planting seeds for tomorrow's vineyard
to reap a harvest called home.

a face of flint
for Malcolm X

there is madness in the atmosphere
thick as the pollution
rotting the air

the world still needs you Malcolm
scared to look into the eyes of your analysis
uncompromising is uncommon these days

and after the towers fell
and Muslims were catching hell
your words were not raised

on whose terms do we live?

how do we learn to

see with new eyes
hear with new ears
speak with new tongues
feel with new hearts

?

I miss you
like I miss my father
with his "give 'em hell son!"

though I never met you
I have dined at the table of your wisdom
I have driven miles listening to your chats
I step to the cadence of your clarity

measure my growth along the rule of your development
I walk with the frustration of Walker
the page soaked with tears
for those willing to accept the chain

too many young bloods
exist in the shadow of your former self
trying to claim the manhood of a slave
dancing between cell blocks
spit bars that keep them on lockdown
incarcerated logic

the chickens keep coming home to roost

those 2-legged dogs who
sniffed your tracks
hounded your footsteps
from Cairo to Paris
and barred you at the gate

are now commonplace occurrences for us of color

but you had a face of flint
chipped away at the plymouth rock that landed on us

we need new direction
leaders with big titles
more eager for popularity than the people
no accountability to the grassroots
we are being choked by the weeds
of our unwillingness to take risks

love is a luxury
lost on the old and the young
hearts apathetic and cynical

diseased arteries of the spirit
we are lost
and too damn stubborn to ask for directions

all the while your spirit
stands behind the podium at the Audobon
pointing forward to freedom

99 Problems & Jay-Z Is Just One
after Jay-Z's rap

a poem of accountability

because of all the rapes
the bruises hid behind make-up or sun glasses
when sistahs aint nuttin but tits and asses
for all the lashes
and the cashes exchanged
because the rates of HIV are souring

for enduring through the attacks
on their character
on their very person

being considered just a booty
and the calls made to the police
for domestic violence
and why women are scared to testify
so they lie through busted teeth
for all the blood spilled
because of Nelly's "Tip Drill"
because women are killed for getting pregnant
by the men who impregnate them

because of all the Black women forced to wet-nurse white babies
while their own children starved

because white women are the only ones this society respects
then blame Black men for imaginary crimes
for the Scottsboro Boys
for the lies that led to lynchings
for being called the bogeyman

and our willingness to play that role
in our very lives

for all the girlfriends, lovers and wives
who sit in prison for defending themselves

because of Bush's attack on Roe v. Wade
because abortion clinics are bombed
for Jefferson raping his slave
and Americans calling that an act of love

because John Wayne called Native American women squaw

because men who think they are above the law
because of the men on the down low

because Snoop Dogg walked onto the stage with women in dog
chains
because of the train
for all the girls raised on gangsta flicks and rap videos
then want to grow up to be a studio ho

because you can't go to college and take a course in fighting
oppression

for all the women Biggie beat down
for why his murderers have yet to be found

because of Hugh Hefner and Howard Stern

because Charles Stewart killed his pregnant wife and blamed it
on a Black man

for all the girls missing and will turn up dead
for their sisters who are scared to go to bed

for all the women forced to sell their bodies just to survive
because women still make less than men

because ministers still preach that women should
obey their husbands
and counsel battered wives to stay with their abusers

because the Southern Baptist Church banned
the ordination of women

because Black youth know more about Foxy Brown
 than Angela Davis

because of the stereotypes
like Aunt Jemima and Sapphire

because of those that blame Eve
and believe that women are made from a man's rib cage

because Sarah Baartman was kidnapped, stripped and caged
and people paid to see her at the World's Fair

because if men had to give birth
we'd all have universal health care

for all the unreported acts of incest

because lil Black boys wanna grow up to be pimps

because no means no
no matter how far she goes

because sex has become synonymous with violence
because love doesn't hurt
because a wife-beater is not a t-shirt

because of Nelly's Pimp Juice

because lil Black girls are called shorties and hotties

until women can walk the streets without being harassed

because R. Kelly videotaped himself
pissing on Black girls
and our community defended him

because of all the men that screamed on Alice Walker
for airing our dirty laundry in the Color Purple

because we have dirty laundry

until domestic workers earn a liveable wage

for those women fighting to keep their family under one roof
because after all this some of yall will still want more proof

because I am not exempt for writing this
because of all the times I have mistreated, yelled or threatened a
woman
cause I refuse to rest until this madness ends

because sexism is as real as racism

and the personal is political
the personal is political
the personal is political
the political is personal.

Identity Theft

they say
imitation is the greatest form of flattery
but I'm not impressed
by those who dress up as the Other
in their attempt to discover
themselves

whiteness is the exclusive club
we Blacks will never get let in
but somehow we supposed to welcome
those who are the beneficiaries of our oppression
dressing up in our darkness

where is the court that will charge them with
identity theft?

this is grand larceny

invaders from outer race
culture raiders
evaders of justice
body snatchers
biting Blackness

aliens in pale skin
invading spaces that are not their own

like the Borg in Star Trek
swallowing whole peoples

cultural germs
white worms

infecting viruses
setting up comfort zones in my home

but no matter how much Blackness you ingest
you can't snatch spirit

the ghost in the machine

the spook in the juke box
cant get got by mere cultural mocking

no matter how shocking

cause
no matter   how long your matted hair/not-locks grow
or how tight your flow
or how many versions of the electric slide or the bump
you know
or how high you can jump
or how long you can hold a note
or how many Black authors you can quote
or how many cowrie shells you rock round your neck
or how fast you can run
or how dark you turn your skin by baking it under the sun
or how fluently you can speak Swahili
or how many times you complement me

you will never know
what it means to be Black

no matter how many trips you make to
Africa or Jamaica or Brazil or India or any other where Black folk
live
you'll never be
anyone other than your white skin privileged self

appreciation is one thing
but appropriation is what you bring
every time you try to sing
and say that you down with the Brown

Blackfolks can't have shit
literally
eventually
you'll see some white folks running up our ass
trying to confiscate our excrement

to rebel against the static whiteness
the blank slate dry and caustic
the caucasian chalk stick
on the global black board

what is it
you can say you own
at the end of yourself
that wasn't taken by force?
of course
you have been trained by the best

what makes what you do
any different than what Columbus did?

imagine him
stealing gold from the Caribs
and raping their daughters
all the while talking bout how
he just love some Carib culture

you need to stop
pause
get behind your
"well see its because"

and reflect on why being white has become so transient and trite
but what is true
is that you
aint challenging
your racism
when you cross the tracks
and enter into that dark taboo

no cops will harass you
you wont be followed in department stores
surveillance cams won't be cramming your personal space

so wigger please
give your tired ass response a rest

cause
our culture is our way of life
is our survival and thrival in a world hostile to our being
it is not a mere cloak
or costume
or tune
or dance
or trance
it is our very existence

you dress up in the vestiges of our darkness
only to take it off when convenient
when it gets too real
when the night stick hits you on your head
and wakes you up to our reality

like that white guy
who tried to discover
what it means to be Black
only to find that he couldn't last a year in our skin

couldn't walk a mile in our shoes

we the ones been bruised
not you
get a clue

see
soul is more than a song
it is a long long history
that you have to live to understand

rather than trying to transcend your whiteness
trace the history of your own race
go find yourself
that pre-white reality
if it can be found
and if it can't
then
go create your own
but whatever you do
leave our shit alone

Bling-Bling
contradictory as Kanye

while your favorite emcee decides how much he'll spend on
bling bling

around the block from Brooklyn
is Kabala in Sierra Leone
home of the diamonds
rocked in rap videos by the very Blacks
whose ancestors started the Middle Passage rhythm
that would become hip hop
but stop!
Pan-African vision been lost
blinded by

the bling bling

the glimmer
the shimmer
the shine
the great white light
but is the price right
when the cost is our very souls on ice

hip hop's paradox

locked in the cell of selling ourselves
as Black
but what gets passed off as that
is a bluff
sold back to us
by those who count their investments
on fingers dipped in our blood

while rap impresarios
mined from ghettoes
serve culture on platinum platters to massa
emcees who can't see
beyond the shine of their diamond-studded teeth
spray lyrical phlegm
like pissin in the dark
keep missin the mark
goin on and on to the break 'a dawn
about murder money and mayhem

minstrels on the world-stage
shot live
from satellite beams
to tv screens all over the globe

but there in the heart of the earth
red core
rivers run in blood like veins
no Jas rule
but real gangstas

here death is not glamorized
in movie sound-tracks by
self-made orphans
after sacrificing their parents
on the altar of diamond warlords who
proffer themselves as gods
and grant their juvenile subjects
the benefits of a slow death

gassing up their bodies in the midst of an
African inferno
inhale cocaine through laced blunts
til their eyes

shot in blood
becomes their vision

to them
bling bling
is not a fashion statement
but a statement to how greed
bring brings
misery to so many

enslaved to America's fascination with shiny rocks

raw and uncut
like the stones
they dive into deep waters searching for
hidden treasure
must grow gills from the sheer will to not drown

and if they come back with nothing but their heartbeats

their punishment is dismemberment

when asked short-sleeve or long
they are not having shirts tailored to fit
but given the choice between life or limb
as the hatchet hovers overhead
while your favorite emcee decides how much he'll spend on
bling bling

tell me
what does Jay-Z have to say
to an African amputee
about a hard knock life
while he rocks the ice
they get sliced for mining a business
they don't own

hands severed
but "diamonds are forever"
how clever
ad campaigns by De Beers
meant to cover the truth

been bamboozled by the bling bling
worthless rocks
hood-winked into thinking these hunks of stone
are precious
which in turn keeps them
omnipotent as Oppenheimer's lust
ground Black bones to dust
making a killing

King Leopold's ghost rocks the stock exchange
in Antwerp in Belgium
home of the soldiers who shot Lumumba
there diamonds are weighed on scales to determine their value
the severed hands of Africa's children serve as counter-weight

how do you calculate the lost of African lives
in carats?

our hearts have grown as cold
as the ice we hock

we are severed from our homeland
separated by more than sea
when we fail to see
our hand in keeping our kin in slavery

while we stand on the auction block
willingly

with our culture in our hands
and our bodies on display

the neon sign above our head reads
slave lotto
50 Cent or a half a buck to play
which is to say
that we are
chained to the desire
to get rich
or die trying

and we are
dying

a slow asphyxiation of our souls
and the whole world watches in utter glee
as we swing from the money tree
with our faces stuck in a Sambo grin

wondering how long they'll have to wait
til we take our last puff
so they can cut off
our hands and eat out our hearts
as precious Black memorabilia

in a refugee camp somewhere between
Russell Simmon's mansion and Patrice Lumumba's grave
an African amputee
daydreams of
American hands frozen with ice
like lice in Cecil Rhode's hair
falling off at the wrist
gangrene
calling that justice

while hobbling on crutches

depraved you say

as you
clutch the pearls of your privilege
and bumrush the stage
dying to become the world's richest ex-slaves.

Burning Still
on the 20th Year Commemoration of the Move Bombing
(May 13, 1985)

a goode for nothing negro
first black mayor of the city
would not become an ambassador
but an embarrassment to his people

playing tough in Rizzo's shadow
plotting death
with feds and city hall gangstas
who call him nigger
under their breath

and to show their barbarity
it was on the day to celebrate mothers
to celebrate life
that the bomb was dropped
on a family that named themselves after the Mother of
Civilization
and an entire block was plunged into hell

and Osage Avenue
became Hanoi in Vietnam

an inferno of heat and lies

the fire dept
became skilled arsonists that day
as they sat on the sidewalk
and watched the block burn
and 11 people inside one home
burn

and we are still burning
and we are still burning
the flames remain
like they do in Tulsa and Rosewood

the fire still rages
in us
the more we learn
the more we burn
with a desire for justice
for righteous retribution

to forgive and forget is not an option
when 9 innocent people still sit in cells
serving the time that should be the punishment
of those that did the crime
of premeditated murder
of a family that loves nature
and blesses the earth
a family that sees the presence of God
in birds, butterflies and human beings
and who are quick to indict devils
who profess humanity
but fail to be humane

keep a record of the names of those
who have put us in these flames

and we do not walk the limp of victims
we stride through the fire as survivors
stronger still
we do not walk alone
but have turned the fire into two torches
one named Ramona
the other Pam

the phoenix of our thirst rises out of the ashes
of the dead
we are moving still
on a Move!
moving still

they cannot make bombs big enough
to blow away our will to live
to be free
to be

so we are rising
rising
still on fire

for this city is still a hell
and good negroes still plot death
under the shadow of white gangstas
who call themselves officials
and pray to Hoover's ghost

in Philadelphia
the city that loves you back
unless you're Black

we know
we know

why the Liberty Bell is cracked

Ewuare Osayande

Purely Victorious
in memory of Ossie Davis (1917-2005)

Act I

what is art
but advocacy

(so said Ossie)

nothing created
that ever was created
was wrought
in a vacuum

all art is made in the real world
where opposites exist and collide

of rich and poor
of less and more
of beauty and gore
of ignorance and lore
of despise and adore
of ill and cure

all art takes sides

whom do you create for?

(so said Baraka via Mao and DuBois)

cant vacillate on the sidelines of life

while the world is backed up against the Wall Street

94

facing the firing squads of imperial goons
and critics
who deify dollars
who reify the status quo
with their front paged lies

who don't know poverty
except as an entry in Webster's dictionary

but we who toil in the defecation of dictators
fertilize an existence from their waste
to indict and defy
those who would have us die

but with each utterance
each manifestation
of our minds

we define for all time

what we see, what we know and we wish to be

the will to free or enslave

if we are conscious or depraved

is carved in the bone of our art

and we are not saved
by it
whether sold or sought

what matters in the end
is the quality of our quest
for beauty and truth

all the rest
is worth no more or less
than the blood
than courses through our veins

Act II

Purlie Victorious
our whole lives are but satires
the enslaved mocking the massa
crackin up under the tracks of tears
that trek down our brown faces
we know more than we let on

sometimes
sometimes

even to ourselves

Act III

and here comes another long-distance runner

race man

carrying the baton passed on by Robeson
he bequeathed to you his vision and voice
and there you stood
smooth chocolate baritone
like a Mingus bass line

(from "II B.S.")
ba doom doom doom doom
da da doimp doimp doimp

da da doom doom doom
da da doom doom doom

doom dippa doom dippa
da da da doom da da doooooommmmm

doimp!

a smooth bluesy
Georgia cotton drawl
spoke in the cadence of dignity
a diction of defiance
to hear you was to hear our history
calling out loud to a future yet to be
to be
to be
to be
to be
true to what we know is so
a steady rhythm of words laced with longing

you constructed verse like a scientist
finding the appropriate weight or measure
you treasured words and the meanings they held

but your most precious gem
was the Ruby you wore around your heart
a courtship of commitment
your marriage was one life-long kiss
the bliss of living on the pulse of purpose
to struggle
to fight
against those that would deny us our love

serenaded by Marian Anderson's contralto
cracking the glass ceiling of whiteness
with the siren of her sincerity

actor with a worker's heart
and hands
carrying our demands to governors
who blocked the doorway to our destiny

you eulogized
both King and the man you called
our Black shining prince
your words covered them like burnt incense
a holy offering
sacred incantations
that can resurrect the dead
still

your shoes cannot be filled
the souls of your feet
88 years thick
double infinity
eternity times two

who will make us live again?

who can speak words
whose truths wont choke them before they leave their mouths?

who can utter a vision then walk it without contradiction?
who can say with you that
"The profoundest commitment possible to a black creator in this
country today—beyond all creeds, crafts, classes and ideologies
whatsoever—
is to bring before his [or her] people the scent of freedom."

I have caught a whiff
from you

Da Mayor

forever saying

"Doctor, always do the right thing"

I've got it.

I'm gone.